Nelson Mandela

Simon Rose

www.openlightbox.com

Step 1
Go to **www.openlightbox.com**

Step 2
Enter this unique code

UYTMDT2RY

Step 3
Explore your interactive eBook!

CONTENTS

AV2 is optimized for use on any device

Your interactive eBook comes with...

Contents
Browse a live contents page to easily navigate through resources

Audio
Listen to sections of the book read aloud

Videos
Watch informative video clips

Weblinks
Gain additional information for research

Slideshows
View images and captions

Try This!
Complete activities and hands-on experiments

Key Words
Study vocabulary, and complete a matching word activity

Quizzes
Test your knowledge

Share
Share titles within your Learning Management System (LMS) or Library Circulation System

Citation
Create bibliographical references following the Chicago Manual of Style

This title is part of our AV2 digital subscription

1-Year K–5 Subscription
ISBN 978-1-7911-3320-7

Access hundreds of AV2 titles with our digital subscription.
Sign up for a FREE trial at **www.openlightbox.com/trial**

Nelson Mandela

Contents

Who Is Nelson Mandela?

Nelson Mandela became the first Black president of South Africa on May 10, 1994, after spending almost 27 years in prison for his political **activism**. In the 1960s, Mandela was a leading member of the African National Congress (ANC). This group fought against **apartheid** in South Africa. Mandela's role in this fight led to his imprisonment in 1964. Even in prison, Mandela was a powerful symbol of the anti-apartheid movement.

After his release from prison in 1990, Mandela worked with F. W. de Klerk, South Africa's president at the time, to end apartheid peacefully. For their efforts, the two men were awarded the **Nobel Peace Prize** in 1993. Shortly after winning this award, Mandela was **elected** to be the next president of South Africa. He retired in 1999. After retiring from politics, Nelson Mandela continued to be an international icon for social justice. When he died in 2013, thousands of people, including more than 90 world leaders, attended his memorial service.

In 1995, South Africa won the Rugby World Cup, the first major sporting event in the country since the end of apartheid. In a moment that symbolized unity within South Africa, Mandela handed the Webb Ellis Cup to team captain Francois Pienaar.

Growing Up

Nelson Mandela was born in the Transkei region of South Africa on July 18, 1918. His birth name was Rolihlahla. Nelson's father, Henry Mgadla Mandela, was the chief of Mandela's town. His mother, Nonqaphi Nosekeni, was the chief's third wife. Nelson was one of 13 children. When he was nine years old, his father died.

Nelson Mandela grew up in the village of Qunu. When not in school, he spent much of his time in the fields, taking care of cows and sheep.

Mandela was the first member of his family to go to school. He initially attended school at a local mission. In 1937, he moved to Healdtown to attend high school. After graduation, Mandela began studying at the University of Fort Hare. This was a top school for Black Africans. Many students from Fort Hare went on to play leading roles in the **independence** struggles of a number of African countries.

Map of South Africa

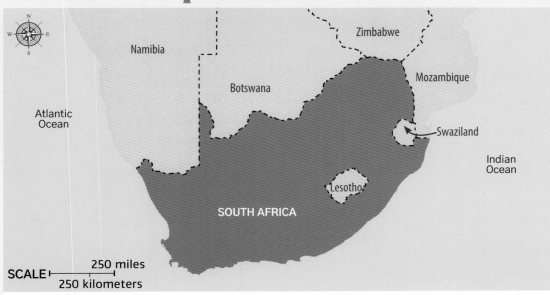

Namibia

Zimbabwe

Botswana

Mozambique

Atlantic
Ocean

Swaziland

Indian
Ocean

Lesotho

SOUTH AFRICA

SCALE 250 miles
       250 kilometers

LEGEND ■ South Africa □ Land □ Water --- Border

South Africa Symbols

TREE
Real Yellowwood

BIRD
Blue Crane

Flower
King Protea

South Africa FACTS

South Africa's population is approximately **60 million**.

South Africa's Table Mountain is more than **260 million years old**, making it one of the **oldest** mountains in the world.

More than **12,000 species** of **plants and animals** live in the waters off **South Africa's coast**.

Practice Makes Perfect

During his first year at the University of Fort Hare, Mandela became involved in a student **boycott**. The students were protesting against the university's **policies**. As a result, Mandela was expelled from the university. He moved to Johannesburg. There, he completed his degree by correspondence through the University of South Africa. At the same time, Mandela worked as a clerk for a law firm. He then studied law at the University of Witwatersrand. In 1944, he joined the ANC.

In 1948, the National Party was elected to form the government of South Africa. This party began the policy of apartheid. By this time, Mandela had been elected as secretary to the youth leadership of the ANC. The ANC Youth Leadership (ANCYL) worked toward securing **citizenship** and voting rights for all South Africans, regardless of **race**.

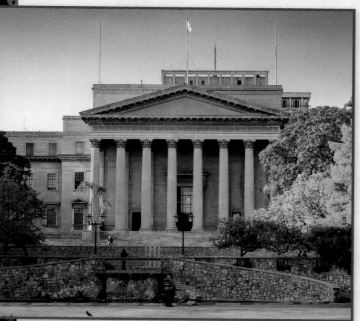

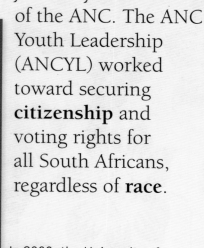

In 2000, the University of Witwatersrand's School of Law opened the Mandela Institute in honor of Nelson Mandela. The institute is known for its work in the area of international economic law.

Mandela became a main figure in the ANC. In 1952, he was arrested for protesting against apartheid. He also took part in a conference called the Congress of the People in 1955. At this event, a document called the Freedom Charter was adopted. Many of the charter's demands were written into the South African **constitution** decades later.

Mandela FACTS

Nelson Mandela won more than **250 awards** for his part in ending apartheid.

More than **25 schools, universities, and educational institutions** have been named after Nelson Mandela.

Nelson Mandela became **president** of South Africa when he was **77 years old.**

A memorial to the Freedom Charter now sits in the South African district of Kliptown, the site of the 1955 Congress of the People. It outlines the changes that those against apartheid wanted for their country.

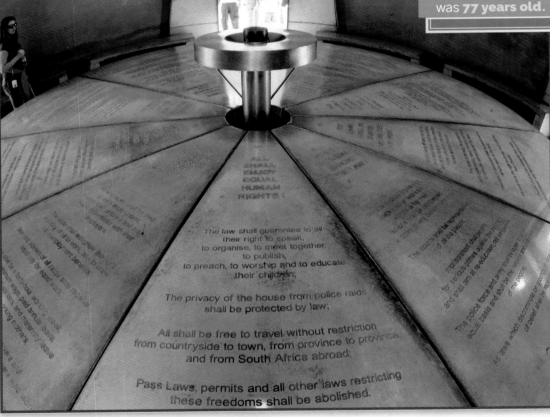

Key Events

During a peaceful protest in December 1956, Mandela and about 150 others were arrested and charged with **treason**. They were accused of trying to overthrow the South African government. Their legal fight became known as the Treason Trial. It lasted until 1961. All those who were arrested were set free.

While the trial was taking place, the Sharpeville Massacre occurred. Police opened fire on a crowd of people protesting South Africa's **pass laws**. About 70 people were killed, and more than 180 were wounded. The Sharpeville Massacre led to the banning of the ANC and other anti-apartheid groups.

After the massacre, the ANC founded a paramilitary group called Spear of the Nation. Mandela was named its commander. He had always supported non-violent protest. However, he knew that a stronger stance had to be taken in the struggle for Black equality. He began campaigning against the government and military. Mandela also left the country illegally. He spoke at conferences and met with other African governments. When Mandela returned to South Africa, he was arrested for leaving the country and sentenced to five years in prison.

The Sharpeville massacre took place on March 21, 1960. Now, every March 21, South Africa holds its Human Rights Day. The day is a time to remember those who fought against apartheid.

Thoughts from Mandela

Nelson Mandela was a champion for the rights and freedoms of people all over the world. Here are some of the statements he made about his beliefs and the lessons he learned in his fight for equality.

Mandela refused to be freed from prison if he had to support apartheid.
"Only free men can negotiate; prisoners cannot enter into contracts."

Mandela stated his views on racism.
"I detest racialism, ...whether it comes from a Black man or a white man."

Mandela showed his commitment to the African people.
"During my lifetime I have dedicated myself to this struggle of the African people. ...I have cherished the ideal of a democratic and free society in which all persons live together in harmony and with equal opportunities."

Mandela spoke about the struggles of fighting for freedom.
"There is no easy walk to freedom anywhere, and many of us will have to pass through the valley of the shadow of death again and again before we reach the mountain tops of our desires."

Mandela discussed the lessons he learned about courage.
"I learned that courage was not the absence of fear, but the triumph over it. The brave man is not he who does not feel afraid, but he who conquers that fear."

Mandela talked about how to make peace.
"If you want to make peace with your enemy, you have to work with your enemy. Then he becomes your partner."

What Is an Activist?

An activist works for a cause. The cause may be to solve a problem or make the world a better place. Political activists, such as Nelson Mandela, seek to bring change to the way people are governed. Other activists may work to protect the environment or help animals. Some activists volunteer for a cause they care about. Others make it their career.

APARTHEID

Apartheid means "apartness" in **Afrikaans**. It was a system of separating people by race. Apartheid was adopted by the South African government in 1948.

Apartheid laws ensured that white people had better treatment than Black people in schools, hospitals, and other public services. Black people were forced from their homes because certain areas were for whites only. They instead had to live in one of ten "homelands." Black South Africans had very few rights and were not allowed to vote.

Activists often plan campaigns to draw attention to their cause. Sometimes, campaigns are aimed at improving people's knowledge of an issue. These are called public awareness campaigns. Other campaigns might urge people to take specific actions on an issue. Nelson Mandela helped launch a campaign of defiance against South Africa's pass laws. He traveled across the country to raise support for this campaign.

Activists 101

Ch'iu Chin
(1879–1907)

Ch'iu Chin was a Chinese revolutionary. She dared to speak out against the powerful emperors who ruled China at the time. She even formed secret societies to try to overthrow them. Ch'iu was captured and tortured, but refused to confess to any crimes. She was then beheaded. The Chinese honor her as one of their great heroes.

Stephen Biko
(1946–1977)

Stephen Biko was a South African anti-apartheid activist in the 1960s and 1970s. He was the founder of the Black Consciousness Movement, an anti-apartheid activist group. Biko died in police custody. Following Biko's death, people gathered to protest the mistreatment he received while in custody.

Ayọ Tometi
(1984–)

Ayọ Tometi is an American advocate for human rights and social justice. She worked with the Black Alliance for Just Immigration, a group that assists immigrant communities, for many years. In 2013, she co-founded the Black Lives Matter platform to combat racism. Its main focus is to uplift Black communities while reducing the violence these communities often face. Ayọ has received many awards for her efforts and continues to work with communities all over the world.

Malala Yousafzai
(1997–)

Malala Yousafzai was born in Mingora, Pakistan, in an area that was controlled by the **Taliban**. The Taliban banned girls from attending school. Malala's father, Ziauddin, ran a school for girls. From a young age, Malala knew that education was important. She spoke out against the Taliban's restrictions on women's education. In 2012, a Taliban gunman attempted to assassinate Malala. She survived the attack, but faced many months of recovery. In 2014, Malala received a Nobel Peace Prize.

Influences

Mahatma Gandhi was a great influence on Mandela. Gandhi is known as the non-violent leader of India's fight for independence. He held protests and demonstrations against British rule from the 1920s until 1948. Gandhi's methods of non-violent protest were known as *satyagraha*. This means "insistence on truth."

Mandela agreed with Gandhi's views on non-violent protest. In January 2007, Mandela attended a conference in New Delhi, India. The event marked 100 years since Gandhi introduced satyagraha to South Africa.

Another important influence on Mandela was American civil rights leader Martin Luther King, Jr. He fought for African American civil rights in the United States in the 1950s and 1960s. King became a leader in the civil rights movement at about the same time that Mandela became a leader in the anti-apartheid movement in South Africa. King believed in non-violent protest. Like Mandela, he was awarded the Nobel Peace Prize. King received the award in 1964 for his work to end racial **segregation** and **discrimination** in the United States.

Gandhi moved to South Africa in 1893. He fought for the rights of Indians there for more than 20 years.

Martin Luther King, Jr. was the president of the Southern Christian Leadership Conference, a group committed to achieving equality through non-violent protest.

THE MANDELA FAMILY

Nelson married his first wife, Evelyn Mase, in Johannesburg in 1944. The couple had four children, two sons and two daughters. The couple divorced in 1958. That same year, Nelson married Winnie Madikizela. They had two daughters, Zenani and Zindziswa. Zindziswa was only four years old when her father was sentenced to life in prison. Nelson and Winnie divorced in 1996. In 1998, at the age of 80, Nelson married Graça Machel. Graça is the widow of the former president of Mozambique, Samora Machel.

Overcoming Obstacles

While serving his five-year prison sentence, Mandela was charged with another crime. He was accused of treason for his role in planning campaigns against the government. This time, Mandela was sentenced to life in prison.

On Robben Island, Mandela was forced to work in the limestone quarries nearby. The light shining off the bright white rocks caused permanent damage to his eyes.

Mandela was first held in a prison on Robben Island. It was located off the coast of Cape Town. Conditions in prison were harsh. Each prisoner had a small cell with a thin mat for a bed and a bucket for a toilet. Black prisoners received the least food. **Political prisoners**, like Mandela, had almost no rights. He was allowed just one visitor and one letter every six months.

In 1982, Mandela was moved to Pollsmoor Prison on the South African mainland. Some people believe he held secret meetings there with the South African government. In 1985, South African President P. W. Botha offered to release Mandela from prison. Mandela had to promise to give up his fight against apartheid. He refused.

While Mandela was in prison, he became known all over the world as South Africa's most important Black leader. People across the globe demanded his freedom. In 1988, Mandela was moved to Victor Verster Prison. There, he lived in a private house. President F. W. de Klerk ordered his release in February 1990.

Nelson Mandela was released from prison on February 11, 1990. Hundreds of supporters greeted him and his wife Winnie outside the gates of Victor Verster Prison.

Achievements and Successes

In 1990, the South African government took the first major steps to end apartheid. That year, the government removed its ban on anti-apartheid groups. This included the ANC. It also released Mandela from prison. Mandela then worked closely with President F. W. de Klerk to end apartheid in South Africa. In 1993, both men were jointly awarded the Nobel Peace Prize for their work toward equal rights for all people in South Africa.

In 1994, Mandela became the first Black president of South Africa. During his five years in office, a new constitution was created for the country. Following his retirement from politics, Mandela continued to work for a peaceful end to conflicts in other parts of Africa. However, in 2004, he retired from public life to spend more time with his family and friends. In November 2009, the United Nations announced that July 18, Mandela's birthday, would be known as "Mandela Day." This day honors Mandela's contribution to freedom around the world.

In 2018, to mark Nelson Mandela's 100th birthday, a life-sized statue of him was unveiled on the balcony where he gave his first speech after being released from prison in 1990.

On December 5, 2013, Nelson Mandela died at the age of 95. His death brought an outpouring of grief and a 10-day period of mourning. Ceremonies were held in South Africa and around the world to pay tribute to Mandela and his accomplishments. He was finally laid to rest on December 15, near his home village of Qunu. Today, millions of people continue to be inspired by his efforts to create a free society.

HELPING OTHERS

One of the first actions Nelson Mandela took as president of South Africa was to establish the Nelson Mandela Children's Fund. The fund aims to create a better future for South African children. The fund supports programs that provide protection and safety for children. It also aims to develop children's individual skills and involve them in the community.

In 2002, Mandela set up another charity, 46664. The charity's name is the prisoner number given to Mandela on Robben Island. It originally began as a charity to bring awareness and work toward the global prevention of HIV/AIDS. The charity has since evolved, and now its purpose is to encourage individuals to fight humanitarian and social injustice.

Write a Biography

A person's life story can be the subject of a book. This kind of book is called a biography. Biographies describe the lives of remarkable people, such as those who have achieved great success or taken important actions

to help others. These people may be alive today, or they may have lived many years ago. Reading a biography can help you learn more about a remarkable person.

At school, you might be asked to write a biography. First, decide who you want to write about. You can choose a political activist, such as Nelson Mandela, or any other person. Then, find out if your library has any resources about this person. Learn as much as you can about him or her. Write down the key events in this person's life. What was this person's childhood like? What has he or she accomplished? What are his or her goals? What makes this person special or unusual?

A concept web is a useful research tool. Read the questions in the following concept web. Answer the questions in your notebook. Your answers will help you write a biography.

Adulthood

- Where does this individual currently reside?
- Does he or she have a family?

Childhood

- Where and when was this person born?
- Describe his or her parents, siblings, and friends.
- Did this person grow up in unusual circumstances?

Your Opinion

- What did you learn from your research?
- Would you suggest these resources to others?
- Was anything missing from these resources?

Writing a Biography

Work and Preparation

- What was this person's education?
- What was his or her work experience?
- How does this person work? What is or was the process he or she uses or used?

Main Accomplishments

- What is this person's life's work?
- Has he or she received awards or recognition for accomplishments?
- How have this person's accomplishments served others?

Help and Obstacles

- Did this individual have a positive attitude?
- Did he or she receive help from others?
- Did this person have a mentor?
- Did this person face any hardships? If so, how were the hardships overcome?

Nelson Mandela Timeline

Nelson Mandela		World Events
Nelson Mandela is born on July 18.	**1918**	World War I comes to an end on November 11, 1918.
Mandela is arrested for demonstrating against apartheid with other ANC members.	**1952**	Dwight D. Eisenhower is elected president of the United States.
Mandela is sentenced to life in prison for treason.	**1964**	The United States Congress passes the Gulf of Tonkin Resolution. This leads to an escalation of the war in Vietnam.
President F. W. de Klerk releases Mandela from prison.	**1990**	Lech Walesa becomes president of Poland.
Mandela becomes the first Black president of South Africa on May 10.	**1994**	The Channel Tunnel opens. It allows people to travel between England and France in just 35 minutes.
The United Nations declares July 18 to be Mandela Day.	**2009**	The United States inaugurates its first African American president, Barack Obama.
Nelson Mandela dies on December 5.	**2013**	Pope Benedict XVI becomes the first pope to resign in nearly 600 years.
Mandela's house is turned into Sanctuary Mandela, a hotel meant for healing and reflection.	**2021**	Joe Biden becomes the 46th president of the United States.

Key Words

activism: action taken to achieve political goals

Afrikaans: the main language of the white rulers of South Africa

apartheid: meaning "separateness" in Afrikaans, this was a system of racial segregation imposed by the South African government until 1994

boycott: to stop using something as a form of protest

citizenship: having rights and responsibilities as a resident of a country

constitution: a document that details the laws of a country

discrimination: treating a person unfairly because of his or her race, gender, age, or physical or mental condition

elected: chosen as a leader by the people in a majority vote

independence: not being influenced or controlled by others

Nobel Peace Prize: an international prize to recognize the person, people, or groups who work toward world peace

pass laws: laws that kept Black South Africans from moving freely within the country

policies: rules and standards

political prisoners: people put in prison for their political beliefs or acts

race: a grouping of people based mainly on physical features

segregation: having separate services and facilities for people of different races

Taliban: a Muslim fundamentalist group

treason: the act of trying to overthrow the government

Index

Get the best of both worlds.

AV2 bridges the gap between print and digital.

The expandable resources toolbar enables quick access to content including **videos**, **audio**, **activities**, **weblinks**, **slideshows**, **quizzes**, and **key words**.

Animated videos make static images come alive.

Resource icons on each page help readers to further **explore key concepts**.

Published by Lightbox Learning Inc.
276 5th Avenue
Suite 704 #917
New York, NY 10001
Website: www.openlightbox.com

Library of Congress Cataloging-in-Publication Data

Names: Rose, Simon, 1961- author.
Title: Nelson Mandela / Simon Rose.
Description: New York, NY : Lightbox Learning, [2023] | Series: History makers : past and present | Includes index. | Audience: Grades 4-6
Identifiers: LCCN 2022001807 (print) | LCCN 2022001808 (ebook) | ISBN 9781791146283 (library binding) | ISBN 9781791146290 (paperback) | ISBN 9781791146306
Subjects: LCSH: Mandela, Nelson, 1918-2013--Juvenile literature. | Presidents--South Africa--Biography--Juvenile literature. | Anti-apartheid activists--South Africa--Biography--Juvenile literature.
Classification: LCC DT1974 .R67 2023 (print) | LCC DT1974 (ebook) | DDC 968.07/1092 [B]--dc23/eng/20220125
LC record available at https://lccn.loc.gov/2022001807
LC ebook record available at https://lccn.loc.gov/2022001808

Printed in Guangzhou, China
1 2 3 4 5 6 7 8 9 0 26 25 24 23 22

022022
101121

Project Coordinator: Heather Kissock
Designer: Terry Paulhus

Photo Credits
Every reasonable effort has been made to trace ownership and to obtain permission to reprint copyright material. The publisher would be pleased to have any errors or omissions brought to its attention so that they may be corrected in subsequent printings. The publisher acknowledges Alamy, Getty Images, Newscom, and Wikimedia as its primary image suppliers for this title.

View new titles and product videos at www.openlightbox.com